D0742958

DATE DUE

THE UNITED STATES

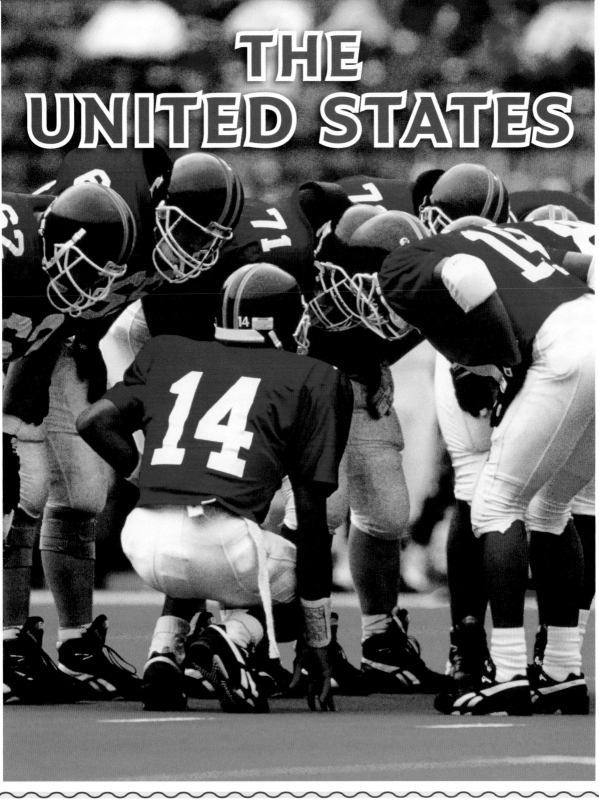

 **Marshall Cavendish**
Benchmark
New York

Written by: Nicole Frank and Elizabeth Berg
Editors: Peter Mavrikis, Cheryl Sim
Publisher: Michelle Bisson
Series Designer: Benson Tan

Photo research by Thomas Khoo

Originated and designed by Marshall Cavendish International (Asia) Pte Ltd
Copyright © 2011 Marshall Cavendish International (Asia) Pte Ltd
Published by Marshall Cavendish Benchmark
An imprint of Marshall Cavendish Corporation
All rights reserved.

This publication represents the opinions and views of the authors based on Nicole Frank and Elizabeth Berg's personal experience, knowledge, and research. The information in this book serves as a general guide only. The authors and publisher have used their best efforts in preparing this book and disclaim liability rising directly and indirectly from the use and application of this book.

Other Marshall Cavendish Offices:
Marshall Cavendish International (Asia) Pte Ltd, 1 New Industrial Road, Singapore 536196 ● Marshall Cavendish International (Thailand) Co Ltd. 253 Asoke, 12th Flr, Sukhumvit 21 Road, Klongtoey Nua, Wattana, Bangkok 10110, Thailand ● Marshall Cavendish (Malaysia) Sdn Bhd, Times Subang, Lot 46, Subang Hi-Tech Industrial Park, Batu Tiga, 40000 Shah Alam, Selangor Darul Ehsan, Malaysia

Marshall Cavendish is a trademark of Times Publishing Limited.
All websites were available and accurate when this book was sent to press.

Library of Congress Cataloging-in-Publication Data
Frank, Nicole.
The United States / by Nicole Frank and Elizabeth Berg.
p. cm. — (Welcome to my country)
Summary: "An overview of the history, geography, government, economy, language, people, and culture of the United States of America. Includes numerous color photos, a detailed map, useful facts, and detailed resource section" — Provided by publisher.
Includes index.
ISBN 978-1-60870-160-5
1. United States—Juvenile literature. I. Berg, Elizabeth, 1953-
II.Title.
E156.F69 2011
973—dc22   2009053767

Printed in Malaysia
135642

PHOTO CREDITS
Alamy: 12, 15 (bottom), 25, 38, 41 (top)
Bes Stock: 23
Corbis: 33 (top)
Dave G. Houser: 3 (top), 5, 8 (bottom), 9 (all), 10, 19
Focus Team: 3 (centre), 22
Getty Images: 11 (bottom), 14, 16, 30, 33 (bottom)
Haga Library: 21, 32 (bottom), 35, 39 (all)
HBL Network: cover, 11 (top), 13, 17, 18, 29 (top), 32 (top)
Hutchison Library: 26, 27, 31 (top)
International Photobank: 2, 4, 7, 8 (top)
North Wind Picture Archives: 3 (bottom), 15 (top and centre), 28, 29 (bottom)
Photolibrary: 1, 6, 20, 24, 34, 36, 37, 40, 41 (bottom), 45
Topham Picturepoint: 31 (bottom)

Contents

Words that appear in the glossary are printed in **boldface** type the first time they occur in the text.

San Francisco's famous trolley cars inch their way up the city's hills.

Welcome to The United States!

The United States is a country of contrasts with crowded cities and small towns, and a wide range of climates and regions. The great size of the United States has always provided new frontiers to explore. Let's learn about the United States and the many different people that populate the country.

Americans enjoy outdoor activities such as camping and fishing in the wilderness.

The Flag of The United States

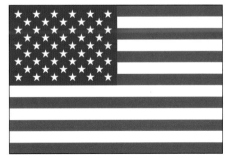

The American flag, called the "Stars and Stripes," was adopted in 1777, when the United States became independent from British rule. The red and white stripes represent America's thirteen original colonies. Each star represents one of the fifty states.

The Land

The fourth largest country in the world, the United States consists of fifty states, including Alaska, to the north of Canada, and Hawaii, which lies in the Pacific Ocean. The forty-eight **contiguous** states cover 2,959,064 square miles (7,663,942 square kilometers). They are bordered by the Atlantic and Pacific Oceans, Canada, and Mexico.

Jackson Lake is surrounded by a breathtaking view of Wyoming's Teton mountain range. The lake and mountains teem with wildlife, including fish, buffalo, antelope, and elk.

The Grand Canyon's majestic gorge was carved out by the winding Colorado River in a process that took millions of years. A natural wonder of the world, the Grand Canyon is 277 miles (446 kilometers) long and 18 miles (29 kilometers) wide. Visitors can drive, hike, raft, and ride mules through the canyon.

The United States has a variety of climates and terrains, including forested coastal plains, the Appalachian Mountains, central plains, the Rocky Mountains, western plateaus, and the Pacific ranges.

The six great rivers of the United States are the Mississippi, Missouri, Ohio, Columbia, Colorado, and Rio Grande. They are used for trade, fishing, **irrigation**, transportation, recreation, and hydroelectric power.

Climate

Climate in the United States ranges from the wet Pacific Northwest to the arid deserts of Arizona, and from the bitter cold of North Dakota to tropical Florida.

Much of the United States enjoys four seasons annually. Alaska, however, is cold most of the year, and the western coast remains mild all year. The southwestern deserts are hot during the day, but cool at night.

Arizona's Sonora Desert is dotted with large cacti, including the saguaro cactus, which can grow to 40 feet (12 meters).

The leaves of **deciduous** trees turn red, orange, and gold in autumn.

The bald eagle, noted for its power and beauty, is the national bird of the United States. Now off of the endangered list, it is still considered a threatened species and lives along rivers and lakes.

Plants and Animals

The United States has a large variety of flora and fauna. The southeastern region is famous for its fruit trees, while the southwestern region has desert-type vegetation. Stunning, giant redwood trees grow along the northwestern coast.

Animals thrive in the American wilderness. Bears live in national parks, and deer inhabit various forested areas.

The Everglades of Florida are packed with plants and animals. Both crocodiles and alligators make their homes in this swampy area.

History

The first inhabitants of North America arrived about 25,000 years ago. European explorer Christopher Columbus arrived in this New World in 1492, followed by colonists who settled the land.

In 1775, the colonists became unhappy with British rule, which led to the Revolutionary War. The colonies declared themselves independent on July 4, 1776. They defeated the British in 1781. General George Washington became the first president.

In the early 1800s, pioneers headed west, traveling in groups along dangerous and unfamiliar trails. These men reenact the pioneers' crossing of the Snake River in Idaho.

Territorial Expansion

In 1803, the United States doubled in size when it bought the Louisiana Territory from France. In 1848, it won the Mexican War, and Mexico handed over land that extended from Texas to the Pacific, including California.

Between 1860 and 1890, about fifty thousand Native Americans were killed by settlers and by diseases. Indians were forced to live on **reservations**, where they have found it difficult to keep native traditions alive.

Railroads transported people and goods across the country, helping the region grow and prosper. Workers celebrate the completion of the first transcontinental railway in Promontory, Utah, in 1869.

The American Civil War set southern states against northern states in a series of battles that cost hundreds of thousands of lives. After four years of fighting, the Confederate states were forced to surrender on April 9, 1865.

Civil War

By the 1850s, the northeastern states were industrialized, while southeastern states were agricultural. African slaves labored on farms and plantations in the south. In 1861, tension between the north and the south led to the Civil War. Four years later, the Union army from the northern states won the war and slavery was abolished.

An Emerging World Power

The United States won control over the new territories of Cuba, Guam, Puerto Rico, and the Philippines in 1898. In 1917, the country entered World War I. A decade of prosperity followed, ending with the 1929 stock market crash and the **Great Depression**. The United States entered World War II in 1941 and emerged as a world power.

World War II was the first time aircraft carriers were used as combat vessels. The USS *Independence* was built after the war and is able to carry more aircraft than earlier models. Today, many carriers have long-range missiles on board.

Fighting the Cold War

After World War II, relations between the United States and the Soviet Union became strained. The two nations entered the Cold War, a period of nonviolent hostility with the threat of nuclear war. The United States actively fought communism in the Korean and Vietnam wars. The Cold War ended in 1991, when the Soviet Union collapsed. Today, the United States exerts great influence in the global economy and in the international community.

The Vietnam War was a time of tension and division in the United States. Many people disapproved of America's involvement in the war and the death of American soldiers.

Thomas Jefferson (1743—1826)

Before his two terms as president, Thomas Jefferson wrote the Declaration of Independence and served as the governor of Virginia, U.S. minister to France, secretary of state, and vice president.

Thomas Jefferson

Abraham Lincoln (1809—1865)

Abraham Lincoln became president in 1860. The Civil War began in 1861. As the country's commander-in-chief, Lincoln helped lead the north to victory. He was assassinated five days after the war ended.

Abraham Lincoln

Elizabeth Cady Stanton (1815—1902)

Elizabeth Cady Stanton helped organize the first women's rights convention in New York. Later, she co-published a newspaper promoting women's rights. Stanton **advocated** co-education and liberal divorce laws.

Elizabeth Cady Stanton

The Government and the Economy

Democracy in Action

A federal democracy was established under the U.S. Constitution. Power is divided between the state and national governments. The executive, judicial, and legislative branches form the national government. Each branch checks the other two to balance power.

President Barack Obama waves to supporters after addressing a joint session of the U.S. Congress.

The U.S. Congress regularly meets at the Capitol Building in Washington, D.C.

The Bill of Rights

The Bill of Rights, the first ten amendments to the Constitution, guarantees Americans certain freedoms, including freedom of religion, speech, and the press. Seventeen more amendments have been added since 1791, for a total of twenty-seven today.

Labor costs are cheaper overseas. To keep manufacturing jobs in the United States, some American manufacturers and foreign competitors have come up with **novel** solutions. For example, at this Toyota plant, a Japanese company, cars are assembled by local American workers and sold domestically.

Economy

The success of the U.S. economy is a result of its **adaptability** to new technologies. In the late 1800s, the country moved from an agricultural to an industrial economic base.

Over fifty years ago, a third of all U.S. employees were factory workers, but during the 1990s, industry declined when cheaper goods from other countries threatened U.S. manufacturing. Services now keep the economy going, and the computer industry continues to grow.

The United States is rich in natural resources. Coal, natural gas, crude oil, iron ore, uranium, gold, and silver are just some of the abundant resources found here.

The United States leads the world in the production of agricultural products. Crops grown in the United States feed the country and one-sixth of the world. Although only 4 percent of Americans work in the farming industry, 43 percent of the land is farmland.

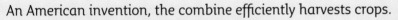
An American invention, the combine efficiently harvests crops.

People and Lifestyle

The American population is over 307 million—30 percent live in cities and 45 percent in suburbs. A decreasing city population has led to **deterioration** in traffic conditions because more and more people commute from the suburbs to workplaces in the cities.

Immigrants from around the world have made their homes in the United States. The population is estimated to grow to 387 million by the year 2050.

A Land of Immigrants

The United States is a land of immigrants, with a variety of races and nationalities. As the country grew, people arrived from all over the world and formed communities of their own, such as Little Italy and Chinatown in New York. Today, most immigrants have adopted an American way of life.

Home Sweet Home

The kitchen's informal atmosphere provides a comfortable place for family members to talk. Barbecues with family and friends are common on weekends.

Most immigrants, such as these women in New York City, have adopted an American way of life.

Public parks are popular places to meet friends, picnic, and play sports. Street performers often entertain the crowds.

Family Time

Most Americans do not live in their hometowns permanently. Many move away when they go to college, find work, or get married. Unlike many other cultures, **extended families** are not as common, and **nuclear families** are the norm.

Many American families now include two working parents. The increasing rate of divorce has also resulted in more single-parent families.

The Road to Adulthood

Individuality is very important in American culture. Young people in America are expected to become more independent as they get older, and they are expected to get part-time jobs to earn spending money. Learning to drive is another step toward independence. Many Americans tend to leave home between the ages of eighteen and twenty-one.

Many Americans enjoy outdoor activities, such as camping and hiking.

Education

American children must attend primary and secondary school. Most students go to public schools. Children attend kindergarten at age five before going on to primary school. Middle school begins in the fifth or sixth grade. High school begins in the ninth grade and goes up to the twelfth grade. Students learn history, reading, science, mathematics, and other subjects. Most students graduate high school at age eighteen.

Kindergarten helps prepare students for primary school.

High school graduation is a very important event for students and their families.

Thirty-four percent of high school graduates attend college. Every state has its own public universities, but there are also many private universities and colleges. An undergraduate degree typically takes four years. Many students return to college to earn an advanced degree.

Religion

Over one thousand religions are practiced in the United States. The Bill of Rights guarantees freedom of religion, and the government does not involve itself in religious matters.

Religious Diversity

Fifty-one percent of Americans are Protestants. Baptists, Lutherans, and Methodists are all Protestants. Roman Catholics make up 24 percent of the population.

Lively singing can be heard in many Baptist church services.

Newfane Congregational Church in Vermont started worship services in 1774. It is one of many small, simple churches built by the first settlers to the New World.

In the nineteenth and twentieth centuries, immigration from Ireland, Italy, and Mexico led to an increase in the Catholic population.

Jews, Muslims, and Eastern Orthodox Christians each represent 3 percent of the population. Islam is growing rapidly in the United States, with 7 million followers.

Language

The basic grammar and usage of American English can be attributed to Noah Webster, who developed American grammar. Webster created a **linguistic** identity based on spoken English. He created new grammatical rules, disregarding many old British English rules.

In 1828, Noah Webster (1758—1843) published *An American Dictionary of the English Language.* He used American spelling in the dictionary.

A Rich Written History

The United States presented an ideal setting for many early American authors. Washington Irving became the country's first short story writer. Edgar Allan Poe, who wrote the poem "The Raven," is famous for his dark, mysterious tales. Herman Melville, Mark Twain, and Henry David Thoreau all excelled at different writing styles.

Ernest Hemingway, William Faulkner, and Toni Morrison have won the Nobel Prize for Literature.

Master Poets

Walt Whitman, Emily Dickinson, T. S. Eliot, Robert Frost, and Maya Angelou have all left their mark on American poetry. Theodore Geisel, better known as Dr. Seuss, is famous for his books for children, such as *The Cat in the Hat*.

Samuel Langhorne Clemens, better known as Mark Twain, wrote several famous books, including *The Prince and the Pauper, Life on the Mississippi, The Adventures of Tom Sawyer*, and *The Adventures of Huckleberry Finn*.

Washington Irving wrote "Rip Van Winkle," a short story about a man who sleeps for twenty years and awakens to find the United States an independent country.

Arts

American Visual Artists

American art was dominated by European influences until 1825. In the early twentieth century, American artists began to express themselves more freely with the use of bright colors, irregular shapes, and different materials. These methods came to be known as modern art, which is also sometimes referred to as avant-garde. After World War II, **abstract expressionism** emerged. Artists explored different styles and techniques of painting. In the 1960s, artists such as Andy Warhol and Jasper Johns used photographs, objects, and other **media** to depict popular culture.

Andy Warhol (1928—1987) was at the forefront of the Pop Art movement, which began as a **criticism** of **commercialism** in American culture. Warhol created bold paintings and experimental films.

Reaching for the Sky

American architect Louis Sullivan created the world's first skyscrapers in the cities of Chicago and New York. Frank Lloyd Wright, famous for designing the Guggenheim Museum, used big, open spaces and **incorporated** the setting into the design. The glass-box look, **post-modernism**, and other architectural styles have also flourished in the United States.

The Chrysler Building in New York City was commissioned by Walter P. Chrysler and built between 1926 and 1930. Its unique stainless steel, sunburst-patterned spire stands out amidst the city's skyline.

The Metropolitan Museum of Art in New York City opened in 1872. It houses American art, as well as important art collections from ancient Egypt, Greece, and the Far East.

Lyrics and Tunes

Ethnic groups in the United States have contributed to American musical history. African Americans provided jazz, blues, and rock 'n' roll. In the 1920s, the descendants of European immigrants who settled in the Appalachian Mountains developed country and western music. One of America's best loved composers is George Gershwin, who wrote *Porgy and Bess*. Broadway in New York City is the home of many famous musicals.

Elvis Aaron Presley was born in 1935. Revered as "The King" of American rock 'n' roll, Elvis died in 1977. His Memphis home, Graceland, is visited by thousands of people every year.

New Orleans' Preservation Hall is a famous jazz club. Jazz tunes, with their characteristic **improvisation**, are never played the same way twice. Duke Ellington, Louis Armstrong, and Billie Holiday are famous jazz greats.

Lights, Camera, Action

Modern cinema originated in the United States as silent movies that captured moving pictures on film. Sound was used in the late 1920s, and in the 1930s, there were **Technicolor** movies. Many film studios sprang up in Hollywood because of the pleasant weather there. Today, it is still the movie-making capital of the world.

The people involved in making movies have also become famous for either directing or acting. Steven Spielberg, Woody Allen, and George Lucas are well known American directors. Famous actors and actresses include Tom Cruise, Will Smith, Reese Witherspoon, and Meryl Streep. Every year, the American Academy of Motion Pictures Arts and Sciences gives out Oscars to the best talents in the film industry. The awards ceremony is broadcast live on television and viewed by millions of people around the world.

Besides movies, Hollywood also produces a variety of television programs. Big names like Warner Brothers, Disney, and Fox started out as film studios, but now include television as a major part of their business.

The world-famous Hollywood sign was first built in 1923 and restored in 1978. Each letter is 45 feet (14 meters) tall.

Philip Seymour Hoffman (**left**), and Reese Witherspoon (**right**) celebrate their Oscar wins for Best Actor and Actress at the 78th Academy Awards in 2006.

Leisure Time

Watching television, cooking, and using the computer are popular American pastimes. Teenagers enjoy spending time going to the movies, the mall, and concerts. Many Americans also enjoy dancing, reading, gardening, traveling, and painting.

Americans like to keep active. Swimming, golf, and tennis are popular sports. During the winter months, children enjoy making snowmen, ice-skating, and sledding.

Americans love camping. This family enjoys a barbecue at a campsite.

Beaches, such as Hawaii's famous Waikiki Beach, attract hundreds of people daily. Popular beach activities include swimming, surfing, volleyball, and picnicking.

Sports Fans

Popular team sports in the United States include baseball, basketball, and football. Many Americans participate in local sports leagues and watch their favorite teams play on television or at a stadium. Millions, for example, follow baseball's annual World Series and football's Super Bowl.

For those who are lucky enough to attend, baseball games are a special treat. Hot dogs, cotton candy, and peanuts are all part of the experience!

Play Ball!

American football is based on English rugby. Baseball evolved from the British game of rounders.

Little League is an organization of baseball teams for boys and girls aged eight to twelve. Most communities have Little League teams, which are supported by the players' parents. Weekend games bring families together.

The National Football League (NFL) currently has thirty-two teams across the country and is the world's largest professional American football league.

Health conscious people in America exercise regularly, both inside and outdoors, engaging in walking, jogging, bicycling, and in-line skating.

The Great Outdoors

The vast outdoors of the United States allows Americans to enjoy leisure activities such as hiking, camping, and canoeing. National parks and public recreational facilities are perfect places for outdoor activities. Highways are often congested on Friday nights when city dwellers head for recreation spots outside the city.

Festivals and Holidays

Independence Day is celebrated on July 4, with picnics and fireworks. Thanksgiving, celebrated in November, began when Pilgrim settlers marked their first year in the New World by feasting with Native Americans.

Christmas, observed on December 25, is a Christian holiday and a time when families sing carols, attend church, and decorate Christmas trees. Easter, another Christian holiday, is celebrated with church, elaborate dinners, and Easter egg hunts.

Holiday spirit is in full swing by Christmastime. Children line up to visit Santa Claus and tell him their Christmas wish lists.

Thanksgiving Day is celebrated on the fourth Thursday of November. Thousands of people attend Macy's Thanksgiving Parade held in New York City, and millions more watch this spectacular yearly event on television.

Carved pumpkins, called jack-o'-lanterns, often light the way for costumed children as they go from house to house collecting candy on Halloween night.

Each ethnic group has its own festivals—Jewish people celebrate Hanukkah, Muslims observe Ramadan, and many African Americans celebrate Kwanza.

Immigrants have greatly influenced American cuisine. Native Americans introduced European settlers to wild game and native plants such as potatoes, corn, tomatoes, coffee, and avocados. English cooking techniques were then used to prepare **indigenous** ingredients. Traditional American dishes incorporate the culinary styles of many immigrant groups.

Most Americans begin their day with a light breakfast of toast or cereal. Pancakes are a favorite breakfast dish. A

Delicatessens sell prepared meats and cheeses. Most of these stores have lunch counters where customers can enjoy hot soup and sandwiches.

typical lunchtime meal includes a sandwich, soup, or salad. Dinner is usually the biggest meal of the day.

Each region of the United States has its own specialties. Many of these specialties are now popular throughout the country. A few regional cuisines include Cajun cooking from Louisiana, Tex-Mex cuisine, which blends Texan and Mexican styles, and Southwestern cooking, which was influenced by Spanish settlers, Native Americans, and cowboys. New England is famous for Boston baked beans and clam chowder.

There are many opportunities to grab a fast meal in the United States. Hot dogs are often sold at sidewalk stands, such as this one in New Orleans.

Served with butter and lemon, lobster is a popular New England dish. Fresh and tasty seafood is caught in the nearby Atlantic Ocean.

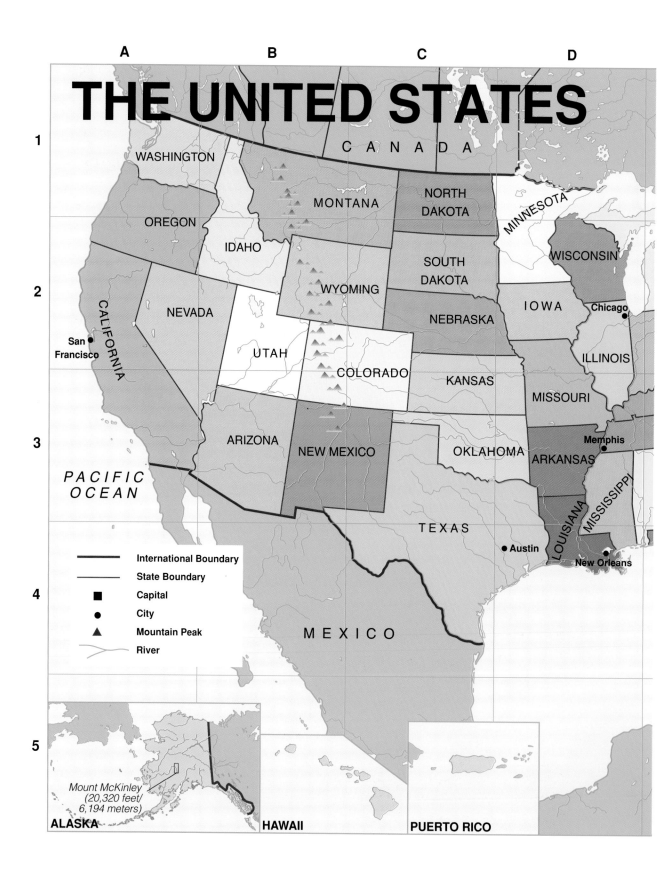

THE UNITED STATES

Alabama E3
Arizona B3
Arkansas D3
Atlantic Ocean F2–F4
Austin D4

California A2–A3
Canada A1–F1
Chicago D2
Colorado B2–C2
Connecticut F2
Cuba E5–F5

Delaware F2

Florida E4

Georgia E3

Idaho B2
Illinois D2
Indiana E2
Iowa D2

Kansas C3
Kentucky E3

Louisiana D4

Maine F1
Maryland F2
Massachusetts F2
Memphis D3
Mexico B3–C5
Miami F4
Michigan E2
Minnesota D1
Mississippi D3
Missouri D3
Montana B1–C1

Mount McKinley A5

Nebraska C2
Nevada A2
New Hampshire F2
New Jersey F2
New Mexico B3–C3
New Orleans D4
New York City F2
New York State E2–F2
North Carolina F3
North Dakota C1

Ohio E2
Oklahoma C3
Oregon A1–A2

Pacific Ocean A3–A5
Pennsylvania E2–F2

Rhode Island F2

San Francisco A2
South Carolina E3
South Dakota C2

Tennessee E3
Texas C3–C4

Utah B2

Vermont F1–F2
Virginia F2

Washington, D.C. F2
Washington State A1
West Virginia E2
Wisconsin D2
Wyoming B2–C2

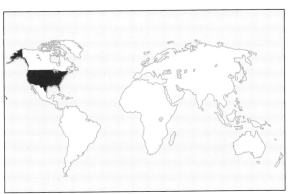

Quick Facts

Official Name The United States of America

Capital Washington, D.C.

Official Language English

Population 307,212,123

Land area 3,537,455 square miles (9,161,966 square kilometers)—all fifty states

States Alabama, Alaska, Arizona, Arkansas, California, Colorado, Connecticut, Delaware, Florida, Georgia, Hawaii, Idaho, Illinois, Indiana, Iowa, Kansas, Kentucky, Louisiana, Maine, Maryland, Massachusetts, Michigan, Minnesota, Mississippi, Missouri, Montana, Nebraska, Nevada, New Hampshire, New Jersey, New Mexico, New York, North Carolina, North Dakota, Ohio, Oklahoma, Oregon, Pennsylvania, Rhode Island, South Carolina, South Dakota, Tennessee, Texas, Utah, Vermont, Virginia, Washington, West Virginia, Wisconsin, Wyoming

Famous Leaders George Washington, Thomas Jefferson, Abraham Lincoln

Currency U.S. Dollar

Many towns in New England date back to before the Revolutionary War.

abstract expressionism: A popular art movement, after World War II, that used patterns and shapes, instead of actual people and objects, to express thoughts and emotions.

adaptability: The ability to adjust to new situations.

advocated: Supported a cause publicly.

commercialism: The practice of making large profits from something, without a regard for quality.

contiguous: Next to or touching.

criticism: The act of expressing disapproval of people or objects.

deciduous: Related to trees that shed leaves seasonally.

deterioration: Worsening. The lowering of value or quality.

extended family: Family group that includes both a nuclear family and other close relatives, all living together in the same household.

Great Depression: A time of terrible economic problems around the world, beginning with the U.S. stock market crash in 1929 and ending with the start of World War II.

improvisation: The act of doing something without advance planning or preparation.

incorporated: Two or more individual parts combined to make one larger unit.

indigenous: Originating in a particular country or place.

individuality: Personal identity. The qualities that make a person different from others.

irrigation: The supply of water by artificial means.

linguistic: Related to language.

media: Means of communication.

novel: New and unusual.

nuclear families: Family groups made up of two parents and their children.

post-modernism: An art movement in the late twentieth century that rejected modern art in favor of more traditional styles and techniques.

reservations: Land set aside for use by Native Americans.

Technicolor: The name of the method that allows movies to be made in full color.

For More Information

Books

Cheney, Lynne. *Our 50 States: A Family Adventure Across America.* New York: Simon & Schuster Children's Publishing, 2006.

Miller, Millie and Nelson, Cyndi. *The United States of America: A State-by-State Guide.* New York: Scholastic Reference, 2006.

Smith, David J. *If America Were a Village: A Book About the People of the United States.* New York: Kids Can Press, Ltd, 2009.

Spengler, Kenneth. *The United States: A Question and Answer Book.* Mankato, MN: Capstone Press, 2007.

Yaccarino, Dan. *Go, Go America.* New York: Scholastic Press, 2008.

DVDs

Drive Thru History: Discovering America's Founders. (Virgil Films and Entertainment, 2009).

Families of USA. (Master Communications, Inc., 2006).

The Founding of America Megaset. (A&E Home Video, 2009).

The History Channel Presents the Presidents. (A&E Home Video, 2005).

Websites

www.colonialwilliamsburg.org/kids/visitUs/#colonialPeople
Explore the lives of colonial Americans in the eighteenth century.

www.gocampingamerica.com/kids/index.aspx
A fun site dedicated to camping, one of America's favorite pasttimes. Includes safety tips, things to look out for, and recipes for the campfire.

www.ready.gov/kids/home.html
The U.S. Department of Homeland Security has created this site just for kids that arms them with useful information about natural calamities and crises, and how to be prepared.

www.socialstudiesforkids.com
An essential source of knowledge on a variety of country-related topics.